The Littlest Dinosaurs

by
Bernard Most

Harcourt Brace Jovanovich, Publishers
San Diego   New York   London

Copyright © 1989 by Bernard Most

All rights reserved. No part of this publication
may be reproduced or transmitted in any form or
by any means, electronic or mechanical, including
photocopy, recording, or any information storage
and retrieval system, without permission in
writing from the publisher.

Requests for permission to make copies of any
part of the work should be mailed to:
Copyrights and Permissions Department,
Harcourt Brace Jovanovich, Publishers,
Orlando, Florida 32887.

Library of Congress Cataloging-in-Publication Data
Most, Bernard.
The littlest dinosaurs/by Bernard Most.—1st ed.
p.   cm.
Summary: Describes some of the smaller dinosaurs, all measuring
fourteen feet or under, in terms of fact and fancy.
ISBN 0-15-248125-7
1. Dinosaurs—Juvenile literature.   [1. Dinosaurs.]   I. Title.
QE862.D5M695   1989
567.9'1—dc19   88-30063

First edition
A B C D E

Also written and illustrated by Bernard Most
DINOSAUR COUSINS?
WHATEVER HAPPENED TO THE DINOSAURS?
MY VERY OWN OCTOPUS
IF THE DINOSAURS CAME BACK

The author wishes to acknowledge the following books as sources
for the factual information contained in the text:
A Field Guide to Dinosaurs by David Lambert
The Illustrated Dinosaur Dictionary by Helen Roney Sattler

The illustrations in this book were done in Pantone markers
on Bainbridge board 172, hot press finish.
Composition by Thompson Type, San Diego, California
Printed and bound by Tien Wah Press, Singapore
Production supervision by Rebecca Miller and Warren Wallerstein
Designed by Nancy J. Ponichtera

To my family,
for their patience and cooperation while I measured just about everything
around our house, including the kitchen sink

I'm sure you know all about the biggest dinosaurs.

I bet you know that brontosaurus (BRON-ta-saw-russ) was more than 75 feet long and that brachiosaurus (BRAK-ee-a-saw-russ) was more than 90 feet long.

You probably also know that ultrasaurus (UL-tra-saw-russ) was the biggest, more than 100 feet long.

But not every dinosaur was so much bigger than you. Would you like to know about the littlest dinosaurs?

Coloradisaurus (kol-or-ADD-ee-saw-russ) was only as long as a seesaw—13 feet.

This plant-eater was used to balancing, because although it walked on all fours, it had to balance on its back feet to reach high leaves.

Ohmdenosaurus (OHM-den-o-saw-russ) was also 13 feet long, about the size of a slide. Even though it was one of the littlest sauropods, it weighed as much as a car.

If you ever see one sliding, make sure you get out of its way.

Bactrosaurus (BACK-tra-saw-russ) was one of the littlest duckbilled dinosaurs. It, too, was 13 feet long — still small enough to fit into a garage . . .

. . . almost.

Scelidosaurus (skel-EE-doe-saw-russ) was 12 feet long, about as long as a diving board. Its heavy body was protected by rows of bony studs, like the earliest crocodiles.

Do you think it could swim like a crocodile?

Coelophysis (see-la-FI-siss) was 10 feet long, a bit longer than a team of Little League baseball players. Scientists think it was able to catch flying insects and flying lizards.

I wonder if it could catch a fly ball?

Dravidosaurus (dra-VID-a-saw-russ) was as long as a bus shelter, about 10 feet.

Even though it was one of the littlest members of the Stegosaurus family, I don't think the bus driver would let it on the bus.

Anchisaurus (ANG-kee-saw-russ) was 8 feet long, but could probably squeeze into a telephone booth. Its fossils have been found all over the world — in North America, Europe, Africa, and Australia.

Don't you think it would like phoning relatives long-distance?

Parksosaurus (PARKS-a-saw-russ) was just 7 feet long, about the size of a bass fiddle. This dinosaur's family lived for over 100 million years, longer than any other dinosaur family.

I think it would have liked the song "Long, Long Ago."

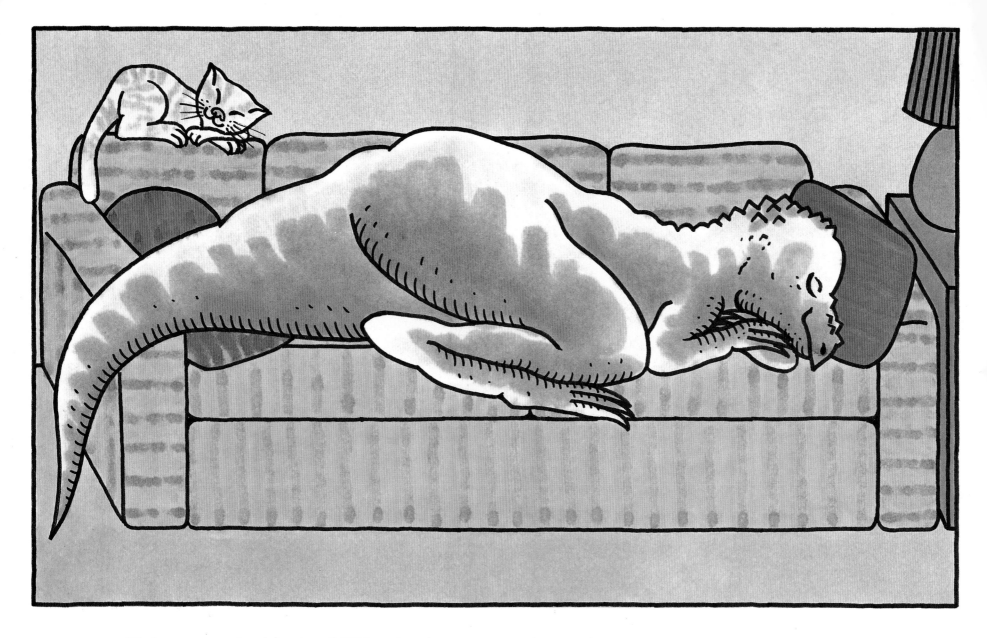

Tylocephale (tie-lo-SEF-a-lee) was 6½ feet long, about the size of a comfortable sofa. This head-butting dinosaur's name means "swollen head."

It might have needed a nap after a hard day of head-butting.

Oviraptor (oh-vee-RAP-tor) was 6 feet long, plenty big enough to raid your refrigerator. Its name means "egg thief"; scientists think it stole eggs from nests.

Do you think it liked dinosaur omelettes?

Stenonychosaurus (sten-ON-ik-a-saw-russ) was about the size of a tall teacher, 6 feet long. It had very large eyes, and scientists think it was the most intelligent dinosaur, because it had a very large brain.

Maybe it could have taught us all about dinosaurs.

Leptoceratops (lep-toe-CER-a-tops) was as long as a dining-room table, just about 6 feet. This plant-eater used its sharp beak for nipping, slicing, and chewing leaves.

Do you think it would have liked spinach and lettuce?

Struthiosaurus (STROOTH-ee-a-saw-russ) was the littlest ankylosaur,
only 5 feet long. It could easily squeeze into the back of a station wagon.
But you would have to find another place for your luggage.

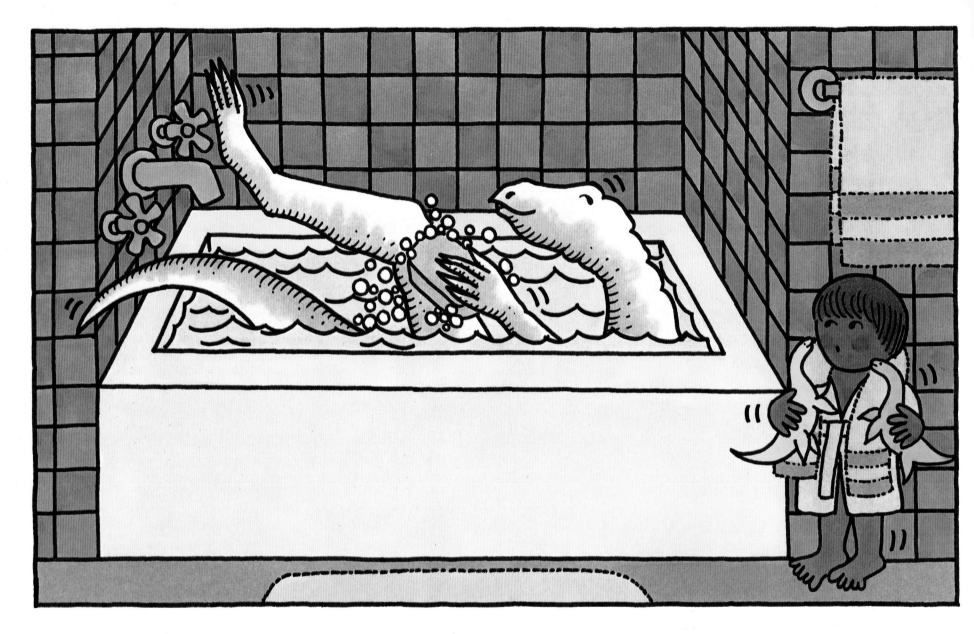

Hypsilophodon (hip-sil-LO-fa-don) was 5 feet long, small enough to slide into your bathtub. Scientists think its five-fingered hands were good for grasping.

But I think it might have trouble holding the soap, don't you?

Lesothosaurus (less-OTH-a-saw-russ) was almost 4 feet long. It could probably fit into many of your clothes, including your sneakers. Scientists think it was a good runner.

Do you think you could beat it in a race?

Tatisaurus (TAT-ee-saw-russ) was the size of a sled, 4 feet long. Like you, it had five fingers and would have kept a strong grip on the sled. If its fingers got cold, would you let it borrow your mittens?

Bagaceratops (bag-a-CER-a-tops) was 3 feet long, small enough to ride a tricycle. Its name means "small horned face," because it had small bumps on its head.

It wouldn't mind falling off and getting another bump.

Othnielia (oth-NEE-lee-ah) was almost 3 feet long, about as big as a toy chest. It was quite an active little dinosaur.
I bet it would like playing with your dinosaur toys.

Microceratops (mike-row-CER-a-tops) was only 2½ feet long. That's just the right size for a pet.

If this little plant-eating dinosaur were my pet, I would nickname it "Mike."

Saltopus (SALT-o-pus) was 2 feet long, little enough to be taken for a ride in a baby stroller.

Of course, you'd have to make sure it wore the seat belt, because it was a very good jumper. Its name means "leaping foot."

Micropachycephalosaurus (mike-row-pak-ee-SEF-a-la-saw-russ) was only 20 inches long.

If you tried spelling its name with blocks, this little dinosaur's name would be much bigger than its body.

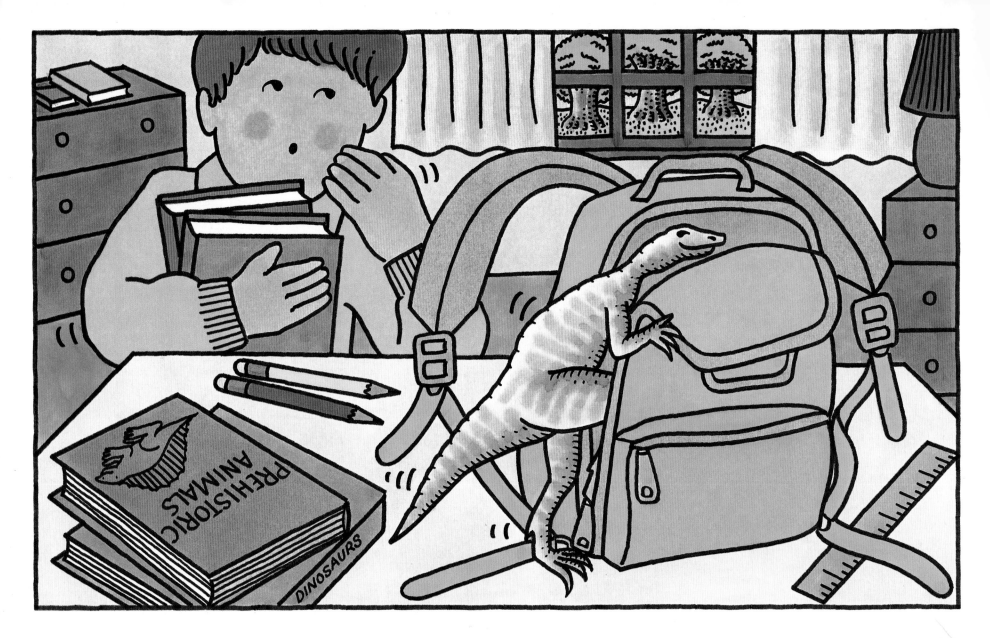

Segisaurus (SEE-gih-saw-russ) was about 16 inches long. This speedy little dinosaur could easily hide inside your book bag.
Wouldn't it be fun to carry it to school to show your class?

The second-littlest dinosaur ever found was a baby psittacosaurus (SIT-a-ka-saw-russ) only 10 inches long, about the size of a cracker box. This "parrot-lizard" had a parrotlike beak.

Do you think it could say, "Psittacosaurus wants a cracker"?

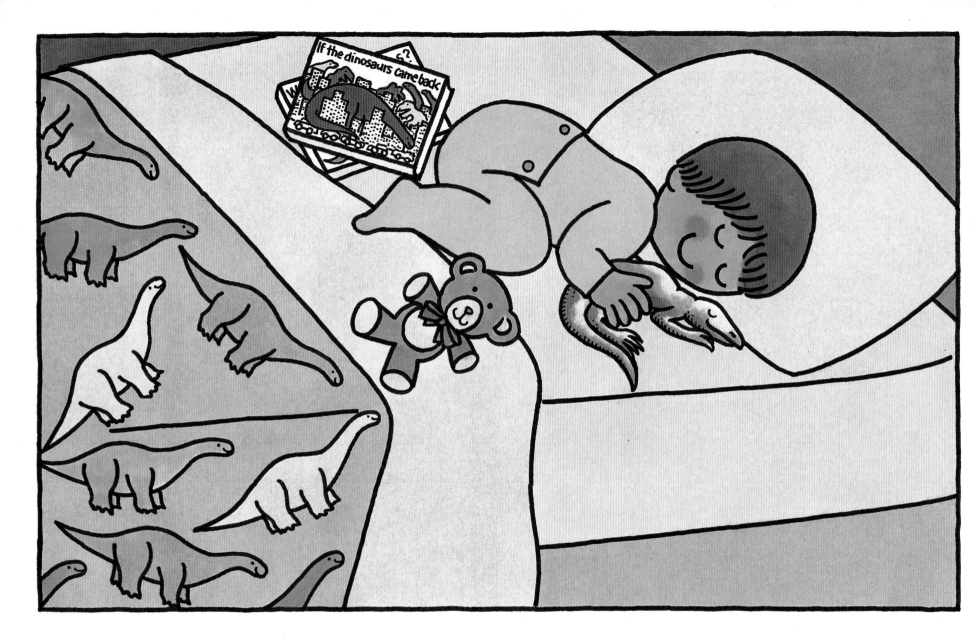

Mussaurus (moo-SAW-russ) is the littlest dinosaur ever found.
It was only 8 inches long, smaller than a teddy bear, but a perfect size
to take to bed.

Do you think it would snore?

Next time you think about the biggest dinosaurs,
don't forget about the littlest dinosaurs.